# Becoming a Butterfly

by Grace Hansen

**abdopublishing.com**

Published by Abdo Kids, a division of ABDO, PO Box 398166, Minneapolis, Minnesota 55439.

Copyright © 2017 by Abdo Consulting Group, Inc. International copyrights reserved in all countries. No part of this book may be reproduced in any form without written permission from the publisher.

Printed in the United States of America, North Mankato, Minnesota.

052016

092016

Photo Credits: AP Images, iStock, Shutterstock

Production Contributors: Teddy Borth, Jennie Forsberg, Grace Hansen

Design Contributors: Laura Mitchell, Dorothy Toth

Cataloging-in-Publication Data

Names: Hansen, Grace, author.
Title: Becoming a butterfly / by Grace Hansen.
Description: Minneapolis, MN : Abdo Kids, [2017] | Series: Changing animals |
    Includes bibliographical references and index.
Identifiers: LCCN 2015959101 | ISBN 9781680805079 (lib. bdg.) |
    ISBN 9781680805635 (ebook) | ISBN 9781680806199 (Read-to-me ebook)
Subjects: LCSH: Butterflies--Juvenile literature. | Life cycles--Juvenile literature.
Classification: DDC 595.78--dc23
LC record available at http://lccn.loc.gov/2015959101

# Table of Contents

Stage 1 . . . . . . . . . . . . . . . . . . . 4

Stage 2 . . . . . . . . . . . . . . . . . . . 6

Stage 3 . . . . . . . . . . . . . . . . . . 10

Stage 4 . . . . . . . . . . . . . . . . . . 18

More Facts . . . . . . . . . . . . . . . . . 22

Glossary . . . . . . . . . . . . . . . . . . 23

Index . . . . . . . . . . . . . . . . . . . . 24

Abdo Kids Code. . . . . . . . . . . . . 24

## Stage 1

All butterflies begin as tiny eggs. Some butterflies lay eggs while flying. Others carefully lay eggs on leaves and other plants.

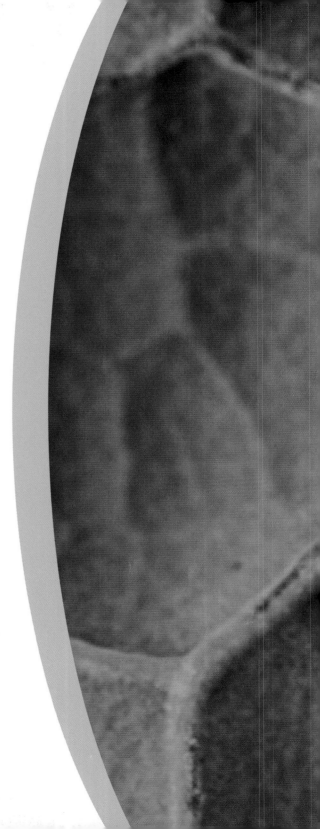

## Stage 2

A butterfly hatches after 7 to 14 days. But it looks nothing like a butterfly! It is a butterfly **larva**, or a caterpillar.

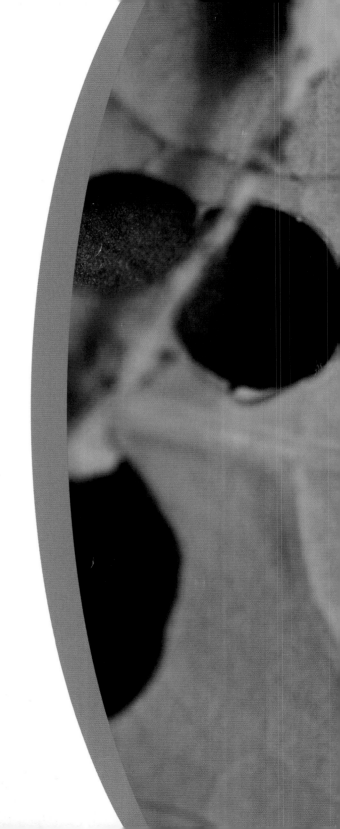

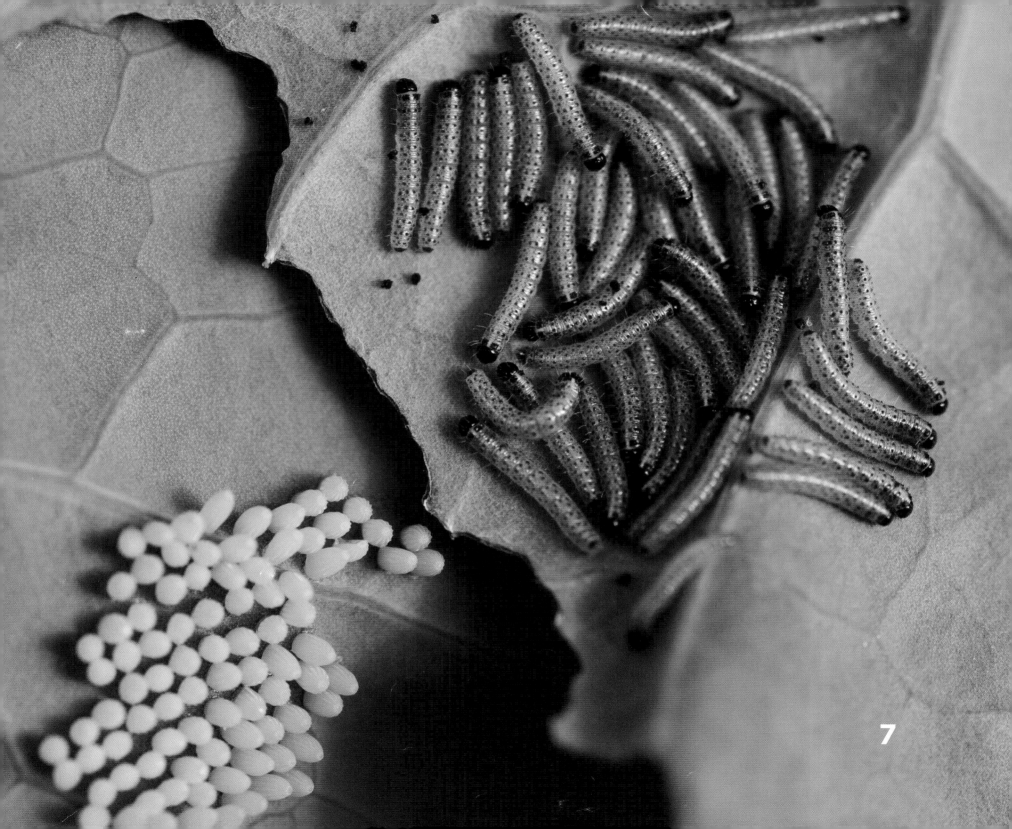

7

The caterpillar is very small.

It has to eat lots of food.

It grows quickly. It sheds

its skin as it grows.

9

## Stage 3

Now the caterpillar is full-grown. It is ready for the next step. It forms into a **pupa**. A pupa is also called a **chrysalis**.

A **pupa** starts as soft and bendable. After a few hours, the pupa is hard. This keeps everything inside safe.

13

The **pupa** does not look like it's doing much from the outside. But there are big changes happening inside!

15

This stage can last between 1 and 40 weeks, depending on the season. Near the end, the **pupa** changes colors. About 3 days later, the butterfly is ready to come out.

17

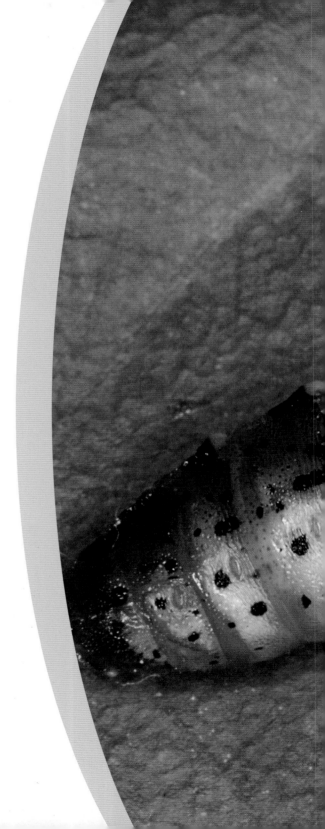

## Stage 4

The butterfly pumps up its body from inside the shell. This splits the **pupa's** shell apart. The butterfly uses its legs to pull itself out.

18

19

The butterfly sends **fluids** to its wings. The wings expand. It takes some time for the wings to dry. Now the butterfly is ready to fly for the first time!

# More Facts

- Some butterflies can taste with their feet. They do this to be sure they can lay their eggs on the leaf they're standing on. Hungry caterpillars will eat the leaf after hatching.

- Butterflies come in all shapes and sizes. The largest butterfly's wingspan can grow up to 12 inches (30 cm)! The smallest grows up to only half an inch (1.27 cm).

- The fastest butterfly can fly 12 miles per hour (19 km/h).

# Glossary

**chrysalis** – the hard-shelled pupa of a moth or butterfly.

**fluid** – a substance, especially a liquid, that is able to flow freely.

**larva** – an active immature form of an insect, especially one that differs greatly from the adult form.

**pupa** – an insect in its inactive immature form between larva and adult.

# Index

adult 18, 20

caterpillar 6, 8, 10

egg 4

fly 20

food 8

hatch 6

larva 6

legs 18

pupa 10, 12, 14, 16, 18

shed 8

wings 20

## abdokids.com

Use this code to log on to abdokids.com and access crafts, games, videos, and more!

Abdo Kids Code:
**CBK5079**